A Word for LENT

a workbook for groups
and individuals

Denis McBride CSsR
Janet Fearns FMDM

Published by Redemptorist Publications
Wolf's Lane, Chawton, Hampshire, GU34 3HQ, UK
Tel. +44 (0)1420 88222, Fax. +44 (0)1420 88805
Email rp@rpbooks.co.uk, www.rpbooks.co.uk

A registered charity limited by guarantee
Registered in England 03261721

Copyright © Redemptorist Publications 2020
First published January 2020

Edited by Janet Fearns
Designed by Eliana Thompson

ISBN 978-0-85231-568-2

A CIP catalogue record for this book is available from the British Library

Excerpts from The Jerusalem Bible, copyright © 1966 by Darton, Longman & Todd, Ltd and Doubleday, a division of Random House, Inc. Reprinted by permission.

Images: p.9: David Shankbone [CC BY-SA 3.0 (http://creativecommons.org/licenses/by-sa/3.0/)]; p.15: סליצ: ילא יבהז ,רפכ רובת [CC BY 2.5 (https://creativecommons.org/licenses/by/2.5)]; p.18: James Tissot, *The Woman of Samaria at the Well*, 1886-1894; p.22: Stephen Broadbent, *The Water of Life*, 1994; p.30: Martinvl [CC BY-SA (https://creativecommons.org/licenses/by-sa/4.0)]; p.37: James Tissot, *The Adulterous Woman Alone with Jesus*, 1886-1894; p.42: Kim Young Gil (1940-2008), *The Crucifixion*, undated.

Every effort has been made to trace copyright holders and to obtain their permission for the use of copyright material. The publisher apologises for any errors or omissions and would be grateful for notification of any corrections that should be incorporated in future reprints or editions of this book.

Printed by Bishops Printers, Portsmouth, PO6 1TR

INTRODUCTION

ach Lent is an invitation; an invitation to come on a journey, a journey with a person, a journey with Jesus. Some readers might remember that in the year of the Millennium, the National Gallery in London opened its doors to a breathtaking exhibition, "The Sacred Made Real". Suddenly the National Gallery was transformed into a sacred space of spontaneous prayer. This was at its most intense in the final room of the exhibition. Gathered around Gregorio Fernández' life-size sculpture, "Dead Christ", visitors stood or knelt in contemplation and communion, in prayer and profound stillness. Past and present intermingled and could not be separated.

A Word for Lent takes us on a similar journey. We have all struggled to make right choices, yearned for others to accept us for who we are, known life-changing moments, celebrated the surprise of undeserved forgiveness and shed tears because we're hurting for one reason or another. *A Word for Lent* invites us to see salvation gradually unfold in our own lives and also in the lives of Gospel women and men whose stories are as relevant today as they were 2000 years ago. We hear their stories and try to make sense of our own. We walk alongside others, past and present, sharing our experience of God, asking questions and praying together as a community of hope. Beautiful works of art accompany us on each stage of our journey through *A Word for Lent*.

Our pilgrimage is helped by the prayer of St John Henry Newman, which perhaps says it all:

> "Stay with me and then I shall begin to shine as you shine,
> so to shine as to be a light to others;
> The light, O Jesus will be all from you;
> none of it will be mine;
> It will be you, shining on others through me."

Enjoy this journey through the Gospels of Lent, and may it be an eye-opening and surprising experience of seeing salvation, perhaps where and when we least expected it.

Fr Chris Vipers
Director of the Agency for Evangelisation
Diocese of Westminster

Ivan Kramskoi, *Christ in the Wilderness*, 1872

Listening to the Gospel

esus was led by the Spirit out into the wilderness to be tempted by the devil. He fasted for forty days and forty nights, after which he was very hungry, and the tempter came and said to him, "If you are the Son of God, tell these stones to turn into loaves." But he replied, "Scripture says: Man does not live on bread alone but on every word that comes from the mouth of God."

The devil then took him to the holy city and made him stand on the parapet of the Temple. "If you are the Son of God," he said, "throw yourself down; for scripture says: He will put you in his angels' charge, and they will support you on their hands in case you hurt your foot against a stone." Jesus said to him, "Scripture also says: You must not put the Lord your God to the test."

Next, taking him to a very high mountain, the devil showed him all the kingdoms of the world and their splendour. "I will give you all these", he said, "if you fall at my feet and worship me." Then Jesus replied, "Be off, Satan! For scripture says: You must worship the Lord your God, and serve him alone."

Then the devil left him, and angels appeared and looked after him.

Matthew 4:1-11

Opening prayer

Heavenly Father,
grant us patience when we are troubled,
gratitude when we are content,
constancy when we are tempted.
Keep us in your everlasting protection,
that we may always wait on you
and never, through any temptation,
be drawn away from you.
Through Jesus Christ our Lord.
Amen.

Listening to life

Take a few minutes to read the following reflection silently or aloud.

Maria genuinely had a headache when she first helped herself to two paracetamol tablets from the drug cupboard on the ward. It didn't take long, however, for her to realise that she could help herself to other items without anybody noticing.

"It's not stealing. Everybody does it", Maria thought as she subsequently slipped a packet of paracetamol into her pocket and ordered a replacement from the pharmacy. Removing ballpoint pens from the drawer at the nurses' station held no difficulties whatsoever. It was even easier to help herself to sticking plasters from the dressing room cupboard: they were invisible in her uniform pocket. A pair of disposable dressing forceps could be "accidentally on purpose" carried from the ward: her son found them useful for arranging his collection of postage stamps.

Maria soon saved money by using the ward's supplies as a ready source of cutlery and toilet rolls: she just hid them in her pocket as she went for her coffee break. Pillow cases and hand towels occasionally found their way from the linen cupboard into her airing cupboard at home. After all, Maria reflected, her need was greater than "theirs" and "they" wouldn't miss the occasional small item from the ward. "It's not stealing. Everybody does it."

Questions for reflection

What is your response to this true story?

If "everybody does it", does that make it right?

Is "everybody does it" a way of escaping responsibility?

Gospel reflection

As you can see from the photograph, the Judean wilderness is no lush Lake District: it's an inhospitable forbidding landscape – from a distance it resembles the cratered surface of Mars. You're not going to go out there for a day's shopping or a cool picnic. The wilderness has a certain majesty about it, but – like a lot of majesty – it's not very homely. Its bearing is too remote, the ground is too hard, the air is too thin and the heat is too oppressive. There are too many rocks, too much light, too little life. Hence Jesus' question to the crowds later on in his ministry: "What did you go out into the desert to look at?"

After forty days in the wilderness, Jesus is tempted to turn stones into bread. In the wilderness Jesus is pulled in two directions: satisfying his present hunger or staying with the hunger for the sake of the mission. He resolves to keep an undivided heart: he will love the Lord and stay faithful to the mission even when his hunger cries out to be answered.

"You shall love the Lord your God with your whole heart."

In the second temptation Jesus is challenged to jump from the highest point in the Temple and land unhurt – because the angels will arrive on time and save him from harm. There is no real danger in this exercise: it appears treacherous only to the uninformed spectator. Thus a spectacular swan dive from the heights that looks deadly dangerous ends up being a theatrical performance that never, for a moment, imperils the subject or involves pain or damage. In this temptation Satan makes a seductive suggestion: that it is possible to love God through theatrical gestures without enduring pain.

9

Jesus has to learn that loving God does not mean exemption from harm. He teaches us that we will be saved; he never tells us that we will always be safe. For Jesus the radical question is: will he continue to love God when his very life is in jeopardy? Will he be able to love God when his body is raised on the cross, and no angel will arrive in time to save him? Will he stubbornly love the Lord through suffering, rejection, and even a violent death?

"You must love the Lord your God with your whole might."

In the third temptation Jesus is on a high mountain and Satan offers him all the kingdoms of the world. The devil offers Jesus immediate power if Jesus will worship him. Why not secure prestige and power now, with instant results, rather than via the tedious route of gathering disciples and followers and winning them to your cause? How long will this venture take and with what results? Better to surround yourself with the guaranteed trappings of absolute authority. You can have immediate status now – no need to wait – and you can lord it over kingdoms.

That idea of lowly service that Jesus will opt for is a long way from Satan's offer ruling over kingdoms. Do you base *your* kingdom on twelve shaky apostles or on the firm ground of real estate? Do you opt for a painless power over people or elect to walk the road of the suffering servant? Do you serve the Lord with what is available to you – that is with your whole soul? Can Jesus do this?

"You shall love the Lord your God with your whole soul."

The temptations give Jesus time to find clarity about himself and his purpose. Sometimes you need your enemy to help you define who you are, what you stand for, and what your governing purpose in life is. Sometimes, paradoxically, it can be your enemy that presses you towards resolution.

Questions for reflection

Can you love the Lord your God with your whole heart, even when you are hungry and forlorn and feel alone?

Can you love the Lord with your whole soul, even when you feel powerless and fragile and have nothing to brag about before God?

Like many persecuted Christians, can you love the Lord with your whole might, even when you face danger and your very survival is threatened?

What can I do?

Pray for all persecuted Christians around the world.

Donate to a food bank and help people who are genuinely hungry.

Final Prayer

We pray for all those who are powerless
to influence their own future;
for all those who are oppressed
in body, in mind, or in spirit.

We pray that whatever forces led them
to the crippling place where they now live,
the Spirit might lead them
out of their address in the wasteland
and give them the courage and strength
to shape their lives anew.

We pray for all those who cannot resist temptation
and who, without intention, destroy their own lives
and bring distress and grief to their loved ones.

We pray for all those addicted to destructive behaviour:
that they might be granted the gift of insight
and the necessary power to choose life again
so they might enjoy peace and serenity in their souls.

We pray for ourselves:
that the Lord might not put us to the test
nor lead us to a time of trial,
but deliver us from all that is evil.

Blessing

May the Lord mark us this day and all our days
with the blessing of his peace.
When we are tired and vulnerable,
may he enliven us with new purpose.
When we are unsure and distrustful,
may he fortify us with new confidence.
When we are depressed and weighed down,
may he raise us to new heights.
Through Christ our Lord.
Amen.

Giovanni Bellini, *Transfiguration of Christ*, c.1480

Listening to the Gospel

esus took with him Peter and James and his brother John and led them up a high mountain where they could be alone. There in their presence he was transfigured; his face shone like the sun and his clothes became as white as the light. Suddenly Moses and Elijah appeared to them; they were talking with him. Then Peter spoke to Jesus. "Lord," he said "it is wonderful for us to be here; if you wish, I will make three tents here, one for you, one for Moses and one for Elijah." He was still speaking when suddenly a bright cloud covered them with shadow, and from the cloud there came a voice which said, "This is my Son, the Beloved; he enjoys my favour. Listen to him." When they heard this, the disciples fell on their faces, overcome with fear. But Jesus came up and touched them. "Stand up," he said "do not be afraid." And when they raised their eyes they saw no one but only Jesus.

As they came down from the mountain Jesus gave them this order. "Tell no one about the vision until the Son of Man has risen from the dead."

Matthew 17:1-9

Opening prayer

Heavenly Father,
we bless you for the gift
of the one you transfigured and called:
"my Son, the Beloved."
You charge us to listen to him.
Help us always to be attentive
to the word of the Lord:
may that word enable us
to look on one another with kindness
and direct the roads we take in life.
This we ask in the name of the Beloved,
Jesus Christ our Lord.
Amen.

Listening to life

Take a few minutes to read the following reflection silently or aloud.

Have you seen the musical "Les Miserables"? Do you remember the child Cosette whose mother, Fantine, left her with an innkeeper's family who were supposed to care for her with the money Fantine earned, first in a factory and then, reluctantly, through prostitution?

Alone, ill-treated and miserable, Cosette sings about her "castle on a cloud" which she visits in her sleep. She dreams that there: "aren't any floors for me to sweep." More importantly, "There is a lady all in white [who] holds me and sings a lullaby. She's nice to see and she's soft to touch. She says 'Cosette, I love you very much.'"

Jean Valjean, an escaped convict, transforms Cosette's life because he rescues her and cares for like the father whom she never knew.

Love makes a difference in real life. How many "ordinary" men and women find that their lives change when they become parents? Did they know in advance that they could show such extraordinary thoughtfulness and generosity? Have they been surprised by discovering their own gentleness, understanding and patience with "the little person" who has entered their lives and homes? Did they suspect that their hearts could almost burst with love for someone else?

Questions for reflection

What is your response to Cosette's dreams of happiness?

Who is the most loving person you know?

What difference has this person made to your life?

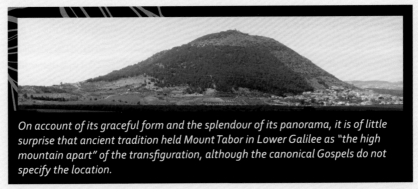

On account of its graceful form and the splendour of its panorama, it is of little surprise that ancient tradition held Mount Tabor in Lower Galilee as "the high mountain apart" of the transfiguration, although the canonical Gospels do not specify the location.

Gospel reflection

TRANSFIGURATION

An old cryptic Chinese saying observes, "You cannot transfigure yourself." I presume it means that something must happen to you or, better still, someone must happen to you, to make you clearly change for the better, so that now you look radiant, shining, and more alive. Something is showing through that wasn't showing through before. Your visible change leads people to wonder. When you walk into a room people notice a difference about you; some might ask, "Whatever happened to you?" The presumption is that something must have happened to you; that you did not organise this transformation yourself; something must have come over you.

While images of Jesus abound in the pages of the Gospel, paradoxically no accurate picture can be formed of him: there is no mention about his physical appearance or the personal details that would be needed to form a reliable likeness of him. Given their subject and their unconcealed devotion, the evangelists are remarkably free of celebrity worship. There is one passage, however, that focuses on Jesus' appearance – when something happens to him on a mountain top and he becomes radiant in the presence of his disciples. We call it the transfiguration of Jesus.

We see Jesus becoming radiant and aglow as he is recognised by God as "my Son, the Beloved". Jesus has had less success in being recognised by others. Because of what Jesus *does* and *says*, people begin asking questions about who he really is. The neighbours think they know: "This is Joseph's son, surely." Others are not so sure. The disciples ask: "Who is this who commands the waves?" Most people reckon that Jesus is more than meets the eye.

Jesus also promotes the question about himself by asking: "Who do people say I am?...Who do you say I am?" These are risky questions to ask because people have a habit of getting the answers wrong! In answer to his questions Jesus is told that he is an ancient prophet come back – like Elijah – or the Messiah who will have victory without suffering. Of course no one will fully know who Jesus is until after the resurrection; but the question is important all the same. Nobody gets the answer right and Jesus goes to the mountain to pray.

In the experience of prayer it is clear that Jesus is not Elijah. Neither is he Moses, the greatest of the ancient prophets. They appear on the scene to direct our attention to a journey Jesus must make to Jerusalem. Peter makes a suggestion that echoes down history: if in doubt, build! But the focus is not on architectural posterity, but on who Jesus is: "This is my Son, the Beloved. Listen to him." Is it any wonder Jesus is radiant and aglow? He has an answer to his prayer. There is someone who gets his name right and that someone is his Father. The deepest part of Jesus is called forth. The Father doesn't just recognise Jesus but *recognises him in love* as his chosen one, and that transfigures Jesus. That recognition is allied to what Jesus must do: being who he is means he must take the road to Jerusalem. And when Jesus comes down the mountain that is what he does: he sets his face towards Jerusalem where he will come face to face with death.

The transfiguration enables Jesus to make the most difficult journey in his life – to take the road that leads to Golgotha.

THE MINISTRY OF TRANSFIGURATION

Transfiguration is not a solitary event in the Gospel but one that happens over and over again. Throughout his public ministry Jesus transfigured many people – the broken, the wounded and the wayward. He called to the deepest part of people and transfigured them by the power of God's love, the same power that transfigured Jesus himself. For Jesus, that experience was getting closer to who he really was. And we all get closer to who we really are when we hear our name called in love. When that happens we become radiant and we are enabled to face the future.

We can understand transfiguration better when we ask: what would it take to transfigure *us*? What would it take to transfigure the people we know? Who calls our name in love? Whose name do we call in love? In our Lenten journey we are asked to transfigure each other by the power of God's love in us. We are all called to the ministry of transfiguration.

Question for reflection

The poet Philip Larkin wrote the following lines.
How do they speak to you?

> In everyone there sleeps
> A sense of life lived according to love –
> To some it means the difference they could make
> By loving others, but across most it sweeps
> As all they might have done had they been loved.

P. Larkin, *The Whitsun Weddings*
(London: Faber & Faber, 1963) 15

What can I do?

Pray for all those people who feel disfigured through lack of being loved.
Can you make someone radiant this week by something you say?

Final Prayer

> We pray for all those who feel defeated by life,
> who believe that life has somehow passed them by;
> we pray for all who are scarred
> in body, in mind, or in spirit;
> for all those who are named and known
> by their affliction or sin.
>
> We pray for ourselves
> that we might never undervalue
> the power of love and attentiveness;
> that we might never harbour our love needlessly,
> nor ignore the little people in life
> who hunger to be noticed and counted.

Blessing

May the Lord look upon us
with kindness and mercy;
may the Lord shine his radiance
upon us and all whom we cherish;
may the Lord keep us forever
in the embrace of his loving gaze.
Amen.

James Tissot, *The Woman of Samaria at the Well*, 1886-1894

Listening to the Gospel

esus came to the Samaritan town called Sychar, near the land that Jacob gave to his son Joseph. Jacob's well is there and Jesus, tired by the journey, sat straight down by the well. It was about the sixth hour. When a Samaritan woman came to draw water, Jesus said to her, "Give me a drink." His disciples had gone into the town to buy food. The Samaritan woman said to him, "What? You are a Jew and you ask me, a Samaritan, for a drink?" – Jews, in fact, do not associate with Samaritans. Jesus replied: "If you only knew what God is offering and who it is that is saying to you: Give me a drink, you would have been the one to ask, and he would have given you living water." "You have no bucket, sir," she answered "and the well is deep: how could you get this living water? Are you a greater man than our father Jacob who gave us this well and drank from it himself with his sons and his cattle?" Jesus replied: "Whoever drinks this water will get thirsty again; but anyone who drinks the water that I shall give will never be thirsty again: the water that I shall give will turn into a spring inside him, welling up to eternal life." "Sir," said the woman "give me some of that water, so that I may never get thirsty and never have to come here again to draw water."

"Go and call your husband," said Jesus to her, "and come back here." The woman answered, "I have no husband." He said to her, "You are right to say, 'I have no husband'; for although you have had five, the one you have now is not your husband. You spoke the truth there."

"I see you are a prophet, sir," said the woman. "Our fathers worshipped on this mountain, while you say that Jerusalem is the place where one ought to worship." Jesus said: "Believe me, woman, the hour is coming when you will worship the Father neither on this mountain nor in Jerusalem. You worship what you do not know; we worship what we do know; for salvation comes from the Jews. But the hour will come – in fact it is here already – when true worshippers will worship the Father in spirit and truth: that is the kind of worshipper the Father wants. God is spirit, and those who worship must worship in spirit and truth." The woman said to him, "I know that Messiah – that is, Christ – is coming; and when he comes he will tell us everything." "I who am speaking to you," said Jesus, "I am he."

At this point his disciples returned, and were surprised to find him speaking to a woman, though none of them asked, "What do you want from her?" or, "Why are you talking to her?" The woman put down her water jar and hurried back to the town to tell the people, "Come and see a man who has told me everything I ever did; I wonder if he is the Christ?" This brought people out of the town and they started walking towards him.

Meanwhile, the disciples were urging him, "Rabbi, do have something to eat." But he said, "I have food to eat that you do not know about." So the disciples asked one another, "Has someone been bringing him food?" But Jesus said: "My food is to do the will of the one who sent me, and to complete his work. Have you not got a saying: Four months and then the harvest? Well, I tell you: Look around you, look at the fields; already they are white, ready for harvest! Already the reaper is being paid his wages, already he is bringing in the grain for eternal life, and thus sower and reaper rejoice together. for here the proverb holds good: one sows, another reaps; I sent you to reap a harvest you had not worked for. Others worked for it; and you have come into the rewards of their trouble."

Many Samaritans of that town had believed in him on the strength of the woman's testimony when she said, "He told me all I have ever done," so, when the Samaritans came up to him, they begged him to stay with them. He stayed for two days, and when he spoke to them many more came to believe; and they said to the woman, "Now we no longer believe because of what you told us; we have heard him ourselves and we know that he really is the saviour of the world."

John 4:5-42

Opening prayer

Almighty God,
in your word to Isaiah you promised:
"The word that goes forth from my mouth
does not return to me empty,
without carrying out my will
and succeeding in what it was sent to do."

Speak to us now your life-giving word
that is never spoken in vain.
Speak, Lord, your servants are listening:
you have the word of eternal life.

Amen.

Listening to life

Take a few minutes to read the following reflection silently or aloud.

Cathy, a scared young student, was about to have her first close encounter with rough sleepers in a shelter for the homeless. For the rest of her life, she would remember the stacked mattresses, stained table and battered chairs. One corner accommodated a sort of cubicle in which a solitary Jesuit lived and cared for the men and women who frequented the shelter.

A man challengingly offered Cathy a cup of tea in an over-sized blue plastic mug. Everyone watched – in silence – until she took her first sip. That was the ice-breaker. Suddenly people were prepared to talk and did so, personally and at great length.

Lunch was Cathy's second big challenge. The Jesuit-prepared stew looked delicious but an elderly woman of questionable hygiene had washed and drip-dried the plates in an even more questionably hygienic cracked washbasin outside the toilet. When had the man who presented Cathy with her plate of food and cutlery last washed his hands? The girl smiled and desperately tried to visualise Francis of Assisi accepting scraps as he begged at people's doors.

Accepting society's marginalised people is often easier in theory than in practice. Sometimes it takes a deep breath and an act of faith.

Questions for reflection

What is your response to Cathy's real-life story?

Why did it make a difference when she had her first sip of tea?

Have you ever had an unexpectedly life-changing encounter with someone?

Stephen Broadbent, *The Water of Life*, 1994

Gospel reflection

When two people meet for the first time they can soon become overwhelmed by the real difference between them – the difference of sex, age, personality, background, religion, nationality, whatever. These differences can all contribute to making the encounter short, sharp and hopeless. The two people might be unable to face each other honestly because the barriers between them seem insurmountable. Nothing will happen unless one of them takes the initiative to overcome the difference between them. Nothing will come of that initiative unless the other person is intrigued into responding.

A man and a woman meet at a well beyond the edge of town. They are strangers – not only because they have never met before but because they should never be meeting at all. He is a Jew who is travelling through foreign territory; she is a Samaritan who is on home ground. Their peoples have been estranged for centuries, and that ancient hostility has been kept alive by each generation. According to their own traditions they should remain strangers. But will this man and this woman allow that estrangement to dictate their attitudes? Will they rise above the mutual hostility of their own traditions and face each other honestly?

JESUS AND THE WOMAN

Of course this is not just any man; for that matter, the Samaritan is not just any woman. In writing the story John is anxious to tell his readers who Jesus is: that he is the Messiah and the saviour of all peoples. But first he shows us Jesus as the weary and thirsty traveller who wants to make inroads into people's lives, no matter who they are. It is Jesus who makes the first move, expressing his need for a drink from her. Thirst knows no boundaries.

The woman is taken aback that a Jew, no matter how thirsty, would bother to ask a Samaritan for a drink. Jesus expects her to be a good Samaritan and his expectation confuses her. He then intrigues her by suggesting that if she knew his real identity she would ask him for living water. The fact that he has no bucket worries her, but the water Jesus has to give turns into a spring inside people. Thinking that Jesus has a cure for thirst, the woman calls him "sir" and now imagines she can avoid trekking to wells in the middle of nowhere.

But Jesus is not talking about making the water authorities redundant. He now focuses on the woman's track record with men. She has a thirst for meeting Mr Right, but the thirst has not been satisfied after five husbands. She is now living with another man. Clearly this woman is familiar with disappointment in love; clearly she is still hoping to meet the right man who can fulfil her deepest needs. Now she is facing a man who is not just another man.

She knows that. She now calls Jesus "prophet". He is a man who knows who she is and yet does not leave her in a heap of pain. He doesn't call her names; he doesn't reprimand her; he merely states how things are. But she moves the conversation on to discuss the proper place to worship God. Jesus is talking about her sex life and she wants to have a seminar on liturgy! When people get too close to where we live, we all want to take a helicopter out of the conversation and move it to a painless, abstract level.

THE WOMAN AS MESSENGER

Jesus follows her cue and talks about the liturgy. But he is not too concerned about the proper address to worship God; he is more concerned that the worship of God be done in spirit and in truth. Jesus leads the conversation back to where it was: the truth. How can you worship God if you don't face the truth about yourself? What kind of cosmetic worship are we talking about that is not linked to who people are and how they are?

So Jesus tells the woman who he is. Jesus is reluctant to admit to his own people that he is the Christ; but he tells this outsider who he is. And in telling her who he is, he gives himself away to her. He gives her the living water – so she can go home without her buckets and jars and face her own people. She leaves him to handle his bewildered disciples while she runs off to tell the town about the man who revealed her to herself.

She does not keep her experience a secret. She turns her experience of Jesus into a message for others. Jesus has freed her to carry his message to others. Because of her the whole town comes to meet Jesus. Many believe in Jesus because of her story; many more come to believe in him when they meet him for themselves.

She is a summary of how people come to understand Jesus: first as a Jew; then as a prophet; then as the Messiah; then as the Saviour of the world. For all the ambiguity of her life, she is one of the first witnesses of John's Gospel who leads others to Jesus. Her past does not hinder her from being a messenger of Good News. She has a story to tell.

At long last she has met the right man.

Questions for reflection

Have you ever not related to another person because of their race or religion or colour?

Would you describe yourself as a wholly unprejudiced person?

What can I do?

Pray for people who feel that they are victims of prejudice.

Today, make an extra effort to be welcoming and courteous to others whether you like them or not.

Final Prayer

We pray for all who are marginalised in life,
for all who are excluded because of their race,
their religion, or their gender:
that they might know the loving embrace of the Lord
who offers them living water,
and experience the acceptance of the community.

We pray for all minorities in every land
who struggle to maintain their own customs
and safeguard their traditional lands.
That they might be seen as a blessing, not a threat;
a gift to the nation, not an embarrassment.

God and Father of all creation,
we bless your holy name,
which you revealed through the Word
you sent among us, your eternal gift,
Jesus Christ, our Lord and God.

He is the way:
through him may we know you and worship you.
He is the truth:
may he reveal your loving plans to us.
He is the light:
may he be a lantern for our steps.

Blessing

May the God who revealed his fullness in Jesus
bless us and keep us close;
may he never withdraw his love from us,
but remember us as the brothers and sisters of Jesus.
This we pray through Christ our Lord.
Amen.

Rembrandt, *Return of the Prodigal Son.* c1667–1669

Listening to the Gospel

he tax collectors and the sinners were all seeking the company of Jesus to hear what he had to say, and the Pharisees and the scribes complained. "This man" they said "welcomes sinners and eats with them." So he spoke this parable to them:

"A man had two sons. The younger said to his father, 'Father, let me have the share of the estate that would come to me.' So the father divided the property between them. A few days later, the younger son got together everything he had and left for a distant country where he squandered his money on a life of debauchery.

"When he had spent it all, that country experienced a severe famine, and now he began to feel the pinch, so he hired himself out to one of the local inhabitants who put him on his farm to feed the pigs. And he would willingly have filled his belly with the husks the pigs were eating but no one offered him anything. Then he came to his senses and said, 'How many of my father's paid servants have more food than they want, and here am I dying of hunger! I will leave this place and go to my father and say: Father, I have sinned against heaven and against you; I no longer deserve to be called your son; treat me as one of your paid servants.' So he left the place and went back to his father.

"While he was still a long way off, his father saw him and was moved with pity. He ran to the boy, clasped him in his arms and kissed him tenderly. Then his son said, 'Father, I have sinned against heaven and against you. I no longer deserve to be called your son.' But the father said to his servants, 'Quick! Bring out the best robe and put it on him; put a ring on his finger and sandals on his feet. Bring the calf we have been fattening, and kill it; we are going to have a feast, a celebration, because this son of mine was dead and has come back to life; he was lost and is found.' And they began to celebrate.

"Now the elder son was out in the fields, and on his way back, as he drew near the house, he could hear music and dancing. Calling one of the servants he asked what it was all about. 'Your brother has come' replied the servant 'and your father has killed the calf we had fattened because he has got him back safe and sound.' He was angry then and refused to go in, and his father came out to plead with him; but he answered his father, 'Look, all these years I have slaved for you and never once disobeyed your orders, yet you never offered me so much as a kid for me to celebrate with my friends. But for this son of yours, when he comes back after swallowing up your property – he and his women – you kill the calf we had been fattening.'

The father said, 'My son, you are with me always and all I have is yours. But it is only right we should celebrate and rejoice, because your brother here was dead and has come to life; he was lost and is found.'"

Luke 15:1-3, 11-32

Opening prayer

Almighty and everlasting God who has revealed yourself
as Father, Son and Holy Spirit,
reigning in perfect unity and love,
we bless you as three persons in one God.

We bring before you all families
who reflect neither your love nor your unity
but who remain stubbornly divided,
haunted by ancient hurts and wounds.

We pray that the members of every family
may be rich in mutual affection and forbearance,
in courtesy and in kindness,
bearing one another's burdens.
Thus may every family reflect something of your love and unity.
Amen.

Listening to life

Take a few minutes to read the following reflection silently or aloud.

Frankie and Tony still had years of their prison sentences ahead of them when they discovered God and their lives changed direction. It wasn't easy. Some of their fellow prisoners were supportive. Others ridiculed them as the pair tried to put God first.

One Saturday morning they walked stiffly and unsmilingly towards the altar, nervously acting tough before their friends who filled the prison chapel to overflowing. Not everybody present was a Christian. Only God, the chaplain and the prison records knew the full range of crimes which the congregation represented and the centuries which were still to pass behind prison bars.

Frankie was baptised; both were confirmed and also received Communion for the first time.

Moments later, thinking themselves unnoticed, a surreptitious smile of pure happiness passed between the two men. Then, at the sign of peace, joy exploded around them as prisoners, chaplains, volunteers and a couple of guards congratulated them with handshakes and bear hugs.

Society remembers the crimes which Frankie and Tony had committed. By contrast, God saw two prodigal sons come home and welcomed them with open arms. The prison community celebrated two people facing a hope-filled future. Their past couldn't change for Frankie or Tony but they had placed their future in God's hands.

Questions for reflection

What is your response to this true story?

When has a change in your life caused you to celebrate?

Have you, or someone whom you know, had a chance to make a fresh start?

Josefina de Vasconcellos,
Reconciliation, 1977

Gospel reflection

SEPARATION ANXIETY

Psychologists tell us that the deepest fear of children expresses itself in separation anxiety – the fear of being abandoned by their parents. Children are afraid that the love which brought them into the world, which names them and claims them, which gives them security, will be withdrawn so that they will end up discarded, disowned and left on the scrapheap. Separation anxiety is the fear of living in the absence of familiar love, of having no place of belonging, of being left at the lost property office, unlooked for and unclaimed.

Of course, we don't have to be geniuses to appreciate that *that* fear is not limited to children. It's part of the baggage of all of us. We all know from experience that there is no such thing as *automatic love*. It is not automatic that a father loves his son, or that a brother loves his brother, or that a daughter loves her mother. We know that when young people leave some homes their absence is not registered as loss, but greeted with relief. They are summed up as being "just a dead loss". Relatives may dismissively say: "Well, he'll be no loss to anyone." For good measure, some are told to do humanity a favour and "get lost".

That attitude of writing people off as lost causes is the problem in chapter 15 of Luke's Gospel. The sinners come to hear Jesus, but the Pharisees and scribes come to complain that Jesus welcomes sinners and eats with them. The Pharisees want Jesus to let the sinners *stay* lost. Why bother with the likes of them? The Pharisees, whose name means "separated ones", see themselves as having no relationship with the sinners. Jesus sees both groups as children of the Father and, therefore, brothers and sisters to each other. Rather than argue the point, Jesus tells a story about a father who has two sons and who loses them both.

The younger son gets lost in a far country while the elder son gets lost staying at home. The younger son leaves home, but his journey leads him to a place of hunger, of degradation and of possible death. He is in danger of dying far away, forgotten and forsaken. But the younger son comes to himself in a pigpen when he realises that he doesn't really belong there, but has a home where he can belong. There's nothing like hunger to sharpen your sense of belonging! The prospect of regular, square meals is enough to head him in the right direction and he makes the journey of return on a full speech and an empty stomach.

All this time his father has not accepted the loss of his son as "just one of those things". His son's being lost has not nullified their relationship: if the son has let go of his father, the father has not let go of his son. He is a father who stays on the lookout, whose eyes hunt the horizon for the return of his son, whose love educates his hope that his son will come back. When he does see his son a long way off he is so moved with pity that he runs to meet him. When someone comes to meet you, your journey is always shorter. The father's love takes the initiative. He meets his son with love's extravagance and, rather than listening to a boring speech, he organises a good party. After all, his son is found.

The elder son is the type who stays out in the fields long after the cows have come home. When he makes his return journey, unlike his younger brother, he doesn't make it to home. His father comes out a second time that day to meet a son but all he gets is another boring speech! "All these years I have slaved for you" shows how the elder brother sees fidelity as slavery. He is enslaved by his own sense of justice. He wants to maintain the estate without any obligations to his brother. He has no reach in him.

In fact *he* is the "separated one" who refuses to recognise his brother as his brother, but is content for him to stay lost. Unlike his father, he cannot surprise his brother with the quality of his mercy. His hard work has made him hard-hearted. As Yeats wrote:

> "Too long a sacrifice
> can make a stone of the heart."

THE BEST IN US

When we look at ourselves we can probably see parts of each of the three characters in us. There is the part of the father in us which has a keen eye for those who are lost and a good nose for when a party is needed. There is the part of the younger son in us which wants to grab everything we can and try everything we shouldn't. And there is the part of the elder brother in us which makes other people pay for our loveless fidelity. All three characters are within us, competing to shape our life. This Lent let's pray that the father in each of us will be fit and willing to run for mercy. After all, there are probably many people in our life who are still a long way off.

Questions for reflection

If you feel comfortable in sharing, is there anyone in your family or community who has got lost along the way or has been isolated?

Have you ever felt cut off or excluded from your family or community? What are the best ways to make people feel welcome?

What can I do?

Pray for all families who suffer from ancient divisions.

Dare you reach out to someone this week who is isolated by their own mistakes?

If there someone in your life who would love to reconnect with you, what could you do?

Final Prayer

For all who give hope to the Church through their leadership of mercy; for all who run to meet the wayward and let them know the welcome of God.

We pray to the Lord.

R: **Give us confidence in your love, O Lord.**

For children who have abandoned their parents and for parents who have abandoned their children; that they may be reconciled one day around the family table.

We pray to the Lord.

R: **Give us confidence in your love, O Lord.**

For all who hunger and thirst for acceptance in our own country; for all who find our country a strange land far from home; that we will meet them with welcome and Christian love.

We pray to the Lord.

R: **Give us confidence in your love, O Lord.**

For all those who do not know how to celebrate with their brothers or sisters; for those who lack nothing but compassion. May they come to know the joy that is in the Lord.

We pray to the Lord.

R: **Give us confidence in your love, O Lord.**

Blessing

May the Lord mark us this day and all our days
with the blessing of his peace.
When we are tired and vulnerable,
may he enliven us with new purpose.
When we are unsure and distrustful,
may he fortify us with new confidence.
When we are depressed and weighed down,
may he raise us to new heights.
Through Christ our Lord.
Amen.

Lucas Cranach the Younger, *Christ and the Woman taken in Adultery*, 1532

Listening to the Gospel

esus went to the Mount of Olives. At daybreak he appeared in the Temple again; and as all the people came to him, he sat down and began to teach them.

The scribes and Pharisees brought a woman along who had been caught committing adultery; and making her stand there in full view of everybody, they said to Jesus, "Master, this woman was caught in the very act of committing adultery, and Moses has ordered us in the Law to condemn women like this to death by stoning. What have you to say?"

They asked him this as a test, looking for something to use against him. But Jesus bent down and started writing on the ground with his finger. As they persisted with their question, he looked up and said, "If there is one of you who has not sinned, let him be the first to throw a stone at her." Then he bent down and wrote on the ground again. When they heard this they went away one by one, beginning with the eldest, until Jesus was left alone with the woman, who remained standing there. He looked up and said, "Woman, where are they? Has no one condemned you?" "No one, sir," she replied. "Neither do I condemn you," said Jesus "go away, and don't sin any more."

John 8:1-11

Opening prayer

Blessed Lord,
for thy tender mercies' sake,
lay not our sins to our charge.
Forgive us all that is past;
give us the grace to amend our lives.

Teach us to be reverent in your presence;
fill our hearts with faith,
our lives with your love,
our days with good works.
May your wisdom be on our lips
and your everlasting kindness in our hearts.
We ask this in your holy name,
Jesus Christ our Lord.
Amen.

Listening to life

Take a few minutes to read the following reflection silently or aloud.

It takes two people to commit adultery, doesn't it? Did the woman brought before Jesus later forgive the coward who had abandoned her to potentially be stoned to death? Did he ever apologise? How did she handle the gossip and contempt after her release?

When someone is the victim of a hit-and-run and experiences life-changing injuries which also affect their family, how easy is it to forgive the driver who escapes justice?

Then there was the man who, backing his car out of the garage, accidentally killed his toddler son who ran into the driveway but couldn't be seen in the rear-view mirror. How long would it be before he could forgive himself? How did his wife cope with the aftermath of the accident?

Forgiveness isn't easy, is it? Not everybody is like the Mizen family, publicly forgiving their son's murderer. In the midst of their agony, the Mizens decided "to look at what is happening when our young people are getting involved in violence." They set up cafés and Safe Havens, places where youngsters can go if they feel they are in danger. Instead of focusing on their pain, the Mizens empower young people. For them, forgiveness is more than "a nice idea": it shows itself in action.

Questions for reflection

What is your response to these true stories?

Why can we sometimes forgive the big things in life but struggle to forgive smaller issues?

Have you ever received or given forgiveness to someone?

How did it feel?

James Tissot, *The Adulterous Woman Alone with Jesus*, 1886-1894

Gospel reflection

NO ONE DESERVES MERCY

The story is told of a young French soldier who deserted Napoleon's army but who, within a matter of hours, was caught by his own troops. To discourage soldiers from abandoning their posts the penalty for desertion was death. The young soldier's mother heard what had happened and went to plead with Napoleon to spare the life of her son. Napoleon heard her plea but pointed out that because of the serious nature of the crime her son had committed he clearly did not deserve mercy.

> "I know he doesn't deserve mercy," the mother answered. It wouldn't be mercy if he *deserved* it."

That is the point about mercy: nobody deserves it. Everyone deserves true justice; mercy, on the other hand, is sheer gift. Mercy cancels out wrongs and transgressions – not because a sparkling defence has been found or excusing causes have been skilfully argued, but because that is the free response of the person who is grieved. Mercy does not suggest that the guilty are not guilty: it recognises the guilt but does not demand satisfaction for the wrong. In all this, mercy reflects the utter graciousness of the one who has been wronged.

MISERY AND MERCY

In this Gospel we have a magnificent story of the mercy of Jesus as he forgives the woman taken in adultery. It is interesting to note that the story is missing from the earliest manuscripts of John's Gospel. Some scholars argue that the delay in accepting the story as part of the Gospel reflects the difficulty many people had in the ease with which Jesus lets the woman off the hook, an easiness which was totally at odds with the strict penitential practices of the early Church. If this is true, it reflects an old problem many people had with Jesus and many people have with God: really believing in what Graham Greene has called "the awful strangeness of God's mercy". Does God forgive as easily as that?

In the Gospel story the woman is caught committing adultery. If it takes two to tango, it takes two to commit adultery, but the man seems to have had ready access to an emergency exit, leaving the woman in the hands of the scribes and Pharisees. These men know the Law of Moses which stated: "If a man is caught sleeping with another man's wife, both must die, the man who has slept with her and the woman herself. You must banish this evil from Israel" (Deuteronomy 22:22). The scribes and Pharisees are zealous about the execution of the Law, which means the execution of the woman. They are in the moral majority, for they clearly have the Law on their side. Thus armed, they come to tackle Jesus on the issue.

Jesus' reaction to all the fuss is to start writing on the ground. But his questioners persist and Jesus responds, not by taking issue with the law, but by taking issue with the lawyers. When you remember the law but forget what the law is for, perhaps your memory is a little selective. Jesus seems to think that all victims can do with some form of allegiance and he refuses to join this moral majority. Jesus does not say that the woman is innocent, or argue that adultery should be taken off the books; but neither is he persuaded about the innocence of her accusers. He asks them to exercise their memories and check their own track record on sin. If any are innocent, they can throw stones. And while they're all having a good think, running their own home videos in their heads, Jesus goes back to his writing.

At least the woman's accusers are honest people, for they readily recognise that they are not innocent accusers. So the procession of unemployed executioners is led away by the eldest – who is no doubt giving the example of necessity! Of course Jesus doesn't want them just to walk away but to exercise their forgiveness too. Jesus and the woman are left alone. As St Augustine described it poetically, "two are left: misery and mercy". And the woman hears good news from Jesus: "Neither do I condemn you... go away, and do not sin any more."

CAUGHT UP IN FORGIVENESS

When we see that Gospel scene we can all imagine ourselves in the place of the woman caught in adultery and probably have no trouble filling in the faces of our accusers who are ready to heave a stone or two in our direction. But that scenario is too easy. The challenge of the Gospel is whether we can see ourselves, not as the woman who is caught in adultery, but as the man who is caught up in forgiveness. Can we forgive as readily as Jesus forgives? Or do we dote on people's wrongdoing, reminding them of past failures, and lighting vigil lamps to their mistakes? Can we forgive and leave it?

We spend time wondering whether God can really forgive without hoarding the hurt. God's track record on forgiveness is clear: God's had lots of practice and God is good at it. How about our track record?

Questions for reflection

In Shakespeare's *The Merchant of Venice*, the moneylender, Shylock, insists on being granted justice before the judge, Portia. She advises him:

> "Though justice be thy plea, consider this,
> That in the course of justice none of us
> Should see salvation: we do pray for mercy;
> And that same prayer doth teach us all to render
> The deeds of mercy."

William Shakespeare,
The Merchant of Venice, Act 4 scene 1

What do you think of this advice?

What can I do?

Pray for all who are caught up in the web of sin or destructive behaviour.

Is there anyone longing for your forgiveness, someone who hurt you in the past and is still enclosed in their wrongdoing? Is it possible for you to say to them: "Neither do I condemn you, go away and do not sin any more"?

Final Prayer

As we bless God our Father for the great deeds he has accomplished in the past let us ask him to open our eyes to see the marvels he is working in our midst.

We pray to the Lord.
R: Deliver us, Lord, from our bondage.

For all who do not know Christ Jesus: that the Lord will show them his face and speak his work so that they can share the supreme advantage of knowing him.

We pray to the Lord.
R: Deliver us, Lord, from our bondage.

For all who share the sufferings of Christ; for those who have lost everything because of their faith; for those who are persecuted for the cause of right. May they too know the power of Christ's resurrection.

We pray to the Lord.
R: **Deliver us, Lord, from our bondage.**

For all who are enclosed in a bitter or hurtful past: that they may experience the power of Christ's forgiveness which does not condemn them but helps them to live in peace.

We pray to the Lord.
R: **Deliver us, Lord, from our bondage.**

Blessing

May the love of the Father enfold us,
the mercy of the Son liberate us
and the fire of the Holy Spirit inflame us.
And may the blessing of the triune God
rest upon us
and abide with us,
now and evermore.
Amen.

Kim Young Gil (1940-2008), *The Crucifixion*, undated

Listening to the Gospel

From the sixth hour there was darkness over all the land until the ninth hour. And about the ninth hour, Jesus cried out in a loud voice: "Eli, Eli, lama sabachthani?" That is: "My God, my God, why have you deserted me?" When some of those who stood there heard this, they said: "The man is calling on Elijah," and one of them quickly ran to get a sponge which he dipped in vinegar and, putting it on a reed, gave it him to drink. The rest of them said: "Wait! See if Elijah will come to save him." But Jesus, again crying out in a loud voice, yielded up his spirit.

At that, the veil of the Temple was torn in two from top to bottom; the earth quaked; the rocks were split; the tombs opened and the bodies of many holy men rose from the dead, and these, after his resurrection, came out of the tombs, entered the Holy City and appeared to a number of people. Meanwhile the centurion, together with the others guarding Jesus, had seen the earthquake and all that was taking place, and they were terrified and said: "In truth this was a son of God."

And many women were there, watching from a distance, the same women who had followed Jesus from Galilee and looked after him. Among them were Mary of Magdala, Mary the mother of James and Joseph, and the mother of Zebedee's sons.

Matthew 27: 45-56

Opening prayer

Lord Jesus, our Redeemer,
who entered into your triumph and glory
by the hard and lonely way of the cross:
may your courage and steadfast loyalty
inspire and strengthen us
to tread firmly the road which love bids us take,
even when it leads to misunderstanding and darkness.
We ask this for your sake,
who endured the way of the cross.
O Lord, be our strength and support.
Amen.

Listening to life

Take a few minutes to read the following reflection silently or aloud.

We all know the unsung heroes and heroines, the uncanonised saints who have transformed the lives of those around them. Those who "blow their own trumpet" have usually done very little for others.

Blessing was amongst the poorest of the poor in Lusaka, Zambia, when a very sick man called out to her. He had seen the tiny bag of dried fish which she had bought for her children's evening meal. It had cost all that had remained of her money. Beyond it, there was nothing. "Please give me your fish," he begged her. "I have not eaten for a few days but I think that I might be able to eat some fish."

Blessing stopped momentarily, knowing that she and her children would go hungry to bed that night, and handed over the bag, in its entirety, to the sick man. She did not look for praise or thanks. She discovered later that she had just given him his last meal: he died a few hours later.

Palm Sunday is about embracing life's challenges without looking for approval. God sees – and that's all that matters. Few people praise the donkey which carried Jesus. Palm Sunday led to Good Friday, but also to Easter.

Questions for reflection:

What is your response to this true story?

Who is your unsung hero or heroine?

Whose example will you always remember?

Francisco de Zurbarán, *Agnus Dei*
(Lamb of God), 1635–1640

Gospel reflection

THE CROSS OF JESUS

We gather to remember the passion of Jesus, to enter its mystery. We gather to hold holy the love that opposed violence and the love that endured violence, the love that made its way with a cross on its back. We gather to profess our gratitude for that love and to stand in solidarity with all those people whose courageous love makes them victims of violence.

The cross of Jesus has not been dismantled; the suffering he experienced has not ceased. The cross stands in the midst of life – not as ritual decoration, but as a reminder that this is the price the world exacts from those who confront its ways with the values of the Gospel.

Could Jesus have avoided the cross? Could he have made a detour around Calvary and continued on his way? Could he not have evaded execution and settled for a quiet existence beside the Sea of Galilee? Did his forgiving love *require* the cross?

JESUS' COMMITMENT

It was not Jesus who looked for the cross; it was the world that looked to the cross as the way to eliminate him. The cross was not the idea of the Father; it was the final solution thought up by a world opposed to Jesus' way. God the Father is not a sadist who planned the destruction of his beloved Son; in letting go of his Son the Father had to be vulnerable to what would happen to his Son at the hands of others. All parents have to take that risk. God the Father, no less, did likewise.

Love does not demand the cross, but in the life of Jesus love ends up on the cross. *That is what actually happened.* That is what continues to happen to self-forgetful love. Love chooses not to avoid the suffering that emerges from its commitment. The avoidance of suffering is not love's governing passion. It cannot be.

Jesus could have avoided going to Jerusalem; he could have taken the advice of the disciples who warned him about the fate that would surely befall him there. But instead of avoiding Jerusalem, Jesus enters it publicly and loudly. He does not disguise himself and slip in through a quiet gate; he heads a parade.

He decides to confront the power that is set against him. And when he chooses to do that, like all people who confront oppression, *he makes suffering visible.* As Theodor Adorno noted:

> "It is part of the mechanism of domination to forbid recognition of the suffering it produces."

Jesus brings suffering to the forefront. For Jesus to have avoided suffering, he would have had to avoid confrontation with the authorities. He would have had to suppress the real suffering of people and settle for the conspiracy of silence. That he refused to do. His love makes itself vulnerable to suffering. He could only have removed himself from suffering by keeping himself untouched by other people's pain, by making himself invulnerable, by removing himself from human relationships. But that was not why he had come. He had not come to be a mobile monument in stone; he was God's love in fragile human flesh and bone. He was God's passion, God's overwhelming love, God's risky adventure.

In the final week of Lent we recall the entry of Jesus into Jerusalem and we hear again the story of the passion. But why should we remember the passion of Jesus? Why keep alive the memory of such anguish and pain? Aren't we supposed to forget about past pain and hurts, and let them disappear if they can?

As Christians we are committed to be a people that remembers the passion of Jesus: "Whenever you do this, do it in memory of me." When a community chooses to remember suffering, its memory becomes a protest. Remembrance of pain demands a future that is more than a repetition of the past. That is why the memory of suffering is dangerous: in recalling the suffering of the victim there is a protest that this should not be repeated again.

That memory also serves to make us aware of the crosses that are in our midst. The memory of Jesus' passion educates us to pay attention to the suffering of others. The cross demands that attention should be paid. So we pay attention to the suffering of Jesus and the suffering of all who are victims of hate and violence.

Questions for reflection

"It is part of the mechanism of domination to forbid recognition of the suffering it produces."

Can you think of modern examples around the world where this is happening?

Can you think of examples where people's protest, making their suffering and hurt visible, has changed their society?

What can I do?

Pray for all those who suffer in silence, for the voiceless who endure oppression and torment.

Give a willing ear to someone who is enclosed inside their own loss or suffering.

Final prayer

We pray for all the followers of Jesus: that we may add our praise of God to the blessings of the ancients, and open wide our hearts to welcome the one who comes in God's name.

We pray to the Lord.

R: **Blessings on him who comes in the name of the Lord.**

For our world, especially for those tempted by violence and bitterness, for those who inflict pain on their neighbour: that Christ will visit them again in his passion.

We pray to the Lord.

R. **Blessings on him who comes in the name of the Lord.**

For all who suffer in the service of others: that their self-forgetfulness and charity will be raised up by the Redeemer of the world.

We pray to the Lord.

R. **Blessings on him who comes in the name of the Lord.**

For ourselves gathered in the name of Jesus: that the passion of the Lord will open our eyes to see again the suffering in our midst, and enable us to bear one another's crosses.

We pray to the Lord.

R. **Blessings on him who comes in the name of the Lord.**

Blessing

May the love of the Father enfold us,
the passion of the Son embolden us,
the fire of the Spirit enliven us;
and may the blessing of God
rest upon us
and abide with us evermore.
Amen.